BREAK OUT!

Getting Past Your Hurts and Start Living Now

By Regina J. King

It Is Possible, LLC

Copyright © 2016 by Regina J. King

All rights reserved.

Book design by Regina J. King

No part of this book may be reproduced in any form or by any electronic or mechanical means including information storage and retrieval systems, without permission in writing from the author. The only exception is by a reviewer, who may quote short excerpts in a review.

This book is based on a true story and actual events. Names, places, and incidents have been changed.

Regina J. King
Visit my website at www.itispossiblellc.com

Printed in the United States of America

First Printing: May 2016
It Is Possible, LLC

ISBN-13: 978-0692674871

To My Mom, Apostle Little, All My Family and Friends, You Mean the World to Me

Table of Contents

Acknowledgement..
Preface..
The Meeting Place...
The Feelings of Intimacy ....
The Demand ....
The Hurt ....
The Compromise ....
Leaving For Good ....
Pack Your Emotional Bags and Go! ....
Soul -Ties ....
I Choose Me ....
Start Living Now...
Living in Limbo ....
 Last Words……………...

Acknowledgement

I would like to take a moment to thank God for giving me the knowledge, wisdom and understanding to know what I had to offer the world. I want to thank a very special person, Apostle Gloria J. Little. You helped in getting what was in me out and on paper. You were the teacher, guide and anchor who helped me put this book together. You are one in a trillion.

Much Love....

Preface

This book is based on a true story. The names have been changed to protect the guilty. There is an issue we deal with on a daily basis called a broken heart. This book is written because it's time for broken relationship problems to be brought to the forefront and dealt with. This subject was chosen because we have deceived ourselves into thinking everything is alright but actually it is not. The hurt and pain we deal with, or have not dealt with, hinders us from our real potential in life. I am motivated to help women and men around the world to be healed from their past hurts and begin living their life now. It's never too late to start over. This book is about a young woman who thought she had found her true love. Only to find out there is more to the story then she thought. A whole lot more! The man she fell in love with was living not a double life but a triple life. Now with a hurting, painful broken heart, she must find her path back to righteousness and begin to live her life again. This book will help women and men pick up the pieces of their broken lives, move forward, and began to live life better than they did before. The emotional process of healing the hurt will take you on a journey that will allow you to heal your hurt once and for all.

I want to thank my family and friends. A special thank you to Apostle Gloria Little. Thank you for your time, mentoring and prayers.

The Meeting Place

HOW WE MET

Have you ever met someone and you thought it was love at first sight? You fell in love with them instantly? You felt in your heart they were someone you could easily spend the rest of your life with? We've all done it at some point in our life. Let me tell you a story of a young woman who had that special encounter.

You know, being a single female in my late 30's, I had it all, or at least, so I thought. I had my career working for a communications company, I had my townhome, I had my own car, and money in the bank. I had arrived! The only thing I was missing was a relationship. I had no one in my life I wanted to spend time with. I didn't go to clubs or really do a lot of socializing. My time would not allow me to socialize and go to gatherings. Between work and church my life was pretty full. I decided to sign up on a dating website. I figured I would see who was out there. I signed up with AOL Match which was the only website available at that time and created my profile. In 1999, dial-up was the fastest and only way to get on the internet. This is what I wrote:

> *"I am a beautiful God-Fearing lady who has a lot to offer. I am a sensual, sexy woman who is well kept. I have no drama in my life because I choose not to have it. I am an intellectual woman*

who has the ability to hold conversations on just about any topic. I love electronics, computers, robotics, artificial intelligence gadgets, etc. I am not your average woman. I like getting out in the yard and working in it. I like fixing things around the house with my man. But don't get me wrong. I know what the man's role is and know how to let him be a man. I know how to dress down but also know how to dress up. I know what needs to be done for every occasion. I do work a lot but I am now ready to meet the right man."

Once I completed my profile with the about me page and pictures, I waited for responses to my page. What did I have to lose? Nothing was going on in my life anyway.

A few days later to my amazement guys were responding left and right. Man, I got excited looking through the messages. Some of the messages were from guys who were an embarrassment to the male species. Others were enjoyable to read. This one guy sent me a message and caught my attention. He was handsome in every way. I immediately responded. We connected and started chatting online. As time went on, we were chatting through the AOL Match website, we decided to try another way to communicate so we found this app called Dial-Pad.

We decided to call each other on the computer using this application. As we talked, it became an everyday affair. I lived in Houston, Texas and he lived in Baton Rouge, Louisiana. We found out we had a lot in common. I loved electronics, he did too. I was business minded, he was also. We talked about everything. From what color was the sky to where we would be in ten years, twenty years. We talked on the computer and then eventually began talking on the phone long distance sharing the bill. We talked so much that it was inevitable that we meet.

We decided one day it was time to meet in person, so in 2000, he came to Houston. I met him in a public place, a gas station, of all places. You can never be too careful when meeting someone you don't know. I told him I drove a red Nissan Sentra. When I got there, I pulled in and parked my car in a well-lit area, this tall light-skinned guy came to my door and opened it. When I saw him close up, OMG, I was in awe. He was clean, well dressed, and muscular. Yes, in great shape.

We reintroduced ourselves and were checking each other out. I promise you, my hormones started racing. We stood there, talking for what seemed like eternity, but it was only about two hours. Neither one of us wanted to leave. It was past 10pm, I told him it would be better for me to go home, because my hormones were out of control.

So, I went home, cooled off and thought about this guy all night. Oh my, I wanted him and wanted him bad. As time went on, we continued to talk over the computer and on the phone. It seemed like everything was working for me. I had started a new job at a prominent financial institution. I was talking to him, it seemed like life was good.

In 2001, it was my birthday and I wanted to do something radical. So my best friend and I with my dog, Gizmo, decided to go to Baton Rouge, Louisiana, so I could see him. We drove up Friday evening, got a hotel room and I waited for him to get off work. When he got home, he called me. I had to sneak out of the hotel room without waking my best friend and my dog. I picked him up and brought him back to the hotel. We sat in the lobby for an hour, talking. He finally got a room and we went to his room. I must admit, I was extremely nervous as to what could possibly happen. In my mind, I wanted to have sex with him. Yes, I said it. It was my birthday and, it's what I wanted as a gift to me. He went into the bathroom and when he came out, he was completely naked. Oh my goodness, did I want him. He started kissing me and the kissing led to other things. Next thing I know, my clothes were off and we were on the bed. I have never had emotions rushing through me the way they were going. I didn't know what was going on. So I said, to hell with it, I was doing it because it was my birthday. Something in me, this faint voice (The Holy Spirit) kept saying don't do it. Of course, I pushed the thought right out of my head. The sex was magical!

I was in another world! He wore me out but, I wore him out too. We ended up falling to sleep together with his arm around me. I felt loved. I felt like I belonged. The best birthday gift I have ever gotten, or so I thought. What a way to go out. Around 30 minutes later, I awoke and realized I was not in my hotel room. I told him I had to leave. I put my clothes on and headed toward the door. When he jumped up, my hormones started racing again. So, I did it again. Yes, I did it a second time. It was good too! He looked like candy waiting to be eaten just standing there. After this second blissful encounter, it was about 4:30am. I told him I had to leave for real this time. We kissed passionately and I left.

My room wasn't far so I tiptoed back into my room, Gizmo was watching the door and saw me come in. Good thing he didn't bark. I got cleaned up and played like I had just woke up. I put on the clothes I was going to wear and just laid down in my bed. My mind was running a marathon. Thinking about what just happened. Thinking, "Did I just do this?" Yes, I did!! And it felt great!!! I wanted to go back, but, knew I could not. After 6am, my best friend and I got up to start packing so we could head to Alexandra, Louisiana. I went to his room to let him know we were about to check out. He was already awake and dressed. So we walked out together and checked out of the hotel. I took him home and we got on the road. A few hours later, we made it to Alexandria. What a ride! He was on my mind the whole trip. What we did, what he said, how I felt. All of it. But then the little voice came (the Holy Spirit) back and started speaking. "You know what you did was wrong. You need to ask for forgiveness." I ignored the voice and kept thinking and doing what I wanted to do. God will let you know when you are heading down the wrong path. He will give you signs. It's up to you to listen and take heed. We talked again later that night, I'm feeling all good and happy. I got nervous every time I talked to him. I would talk to him when I got up in the morning and he's the last one I talked to before I went to sleep. I was tied to him in every way.

The Feelings of Intimacy

WHAT IS THIS I'M FEELING?

As time passed, we didn't see each other again until 2004. Time flies when you're having fun and when you're happy. Because of the distance, it had been a few years, but we talked every day. He became a part of my daily routine. He decided to visit Houston again and I was ready. Boy oh boy, was I happy. It's been three years and the excitement and anticipation was killing me. This overwhelming feeling of me wanting him. I felt like I needed him and must have him. What is this? Is it love? Is it infatuation? Or is it lust? I'm not use to these emotions. The knotting in the stomach feeling, the perspiration from just the thought of him. This is all new to me. If I had my way, I would move to Baton Rouge. However, he said he was thinking about moving to Houston. That would be ideal.

EMOTIONAL TIES

When he arrived, he called me and told me where he was staying. So, out the door I go. Things were running through my mind. What I was feeling and what I wanted to do. I really wanted to be with him, by any means necessary.

I feel like I was addicted to him. It seemed like everything he did affected me. I felt like he was "Simon Says..." and I was the puppet that complied. When I saw him, it was wonderful! No sooner than I walked through the thresh hole of the door, I was in his arms. The passion behind the kissing, the touching and caressing made me feel like I was the most important person in his life. The feeling of intimacy was in the air. I just knew I had fallen for this guy. I had fallen in love. He had me, all of me. The emotional ties were so strong for me to control, I just couldn't get enough of him. I couldn't get enough of the way he smelled, the way he felt, his touch, I was addicted. I was completely drawn to him. We made love for hours. It was awesome. I felt safe with him. Afterward we talked about the future, about him moving to Houston, we talked about everything. I felt like anything he would say to me, I would do it. I was under his spell. Again this voice (the Holy Spirit) was in my head saying, "This is wrong, he is not your husband. You are not in a committed relationship. You must stop this." Once again, I ignored and pushed it out of my head. Something has changed in me. It's like I have no boundaries with him. Something had gotten a hold of me. And it won't let me go and I didn't want to be let go either.

MENTAL TIES

I began to build my life around him. Saying, "When he moves to Houston, he can stay with me. We can get married and start a life together. We would build an empire." I had it all figured out, the whole nine yards. I was ready!!! Spending time with him made me realize he was the only one for me. I didn't want anyone nor did I have a desire for anyone else. He was the one, the only one.

After a few days, he left to go back home. I missed him already. He was always on my mind. He had me so tied up mentally, I couldn't think about anything or anyone else. Have you ever been so wrapped up in someone, you couldn't think straight? He was all intertwined in my mind. He had become a part of me. I was all messed up inside. I would be at work and think about him and would become all moist and wet. The visions would play in my mind over, and over, and over again. I would be in church, standing with the praise team singing and the vision would pop up in my head. I would try to shake it off, it was too strong. While listening to the sermon, they would appear again, I'd have to fight the images off. It was getting out of control. It didn't matter where I was, the images and movie clips would play in my head. Once again this soft voice (the Holy Spirit) said, "I told you this was not good. You must stop this because it's getting out of hand."

SPIRITUAL TIES

I tell you what, when you're tied to someone that deep, it can become damaging. He had my heart, mind, body and soul tied with him. I gave up my complete self to another human being.

Crazy!!!! But I did. I had it bad, for real! I only saw him every couple of years but my emotions were already involved. My spirit was tied to him. I didn't realize how much until I started changing the way I acted toward other people. Things I said I would never do, I started contemplating doing them. You now the things I'm speaking of. Words coming out of my mouth I would never say normally.

Things I would normally frown upon, here I am thinking of those things. What is going on in my head, my heart, my body and my soul? It is a good thing I didn't see him but every once in a while. It would be damaging to me if I was in constant physical contact with him. I would be at church but would not be attentive like I used to be. I was there physically but not spiritually, I would be impatient of my time there and wondering what he was doing. I noticed I could not praise God the way I used to, things started changing, I started changing. And it was not for the good. A part of me felt like I was in a dark hole. Again, this voice (the Holy Spirit) spoke, "You are in over your head. You have to stop before it's too late." "Nope!" I said. I liked what I was feeling, I liked what I was doing. Now there was an all-out war going on with my spirit and my flesh. I stopped reading and studying the bible. I played a great role, should have won an Oscar for the starring role of the church hypocrite or the backslider. Even though all of this was going on with me, I still wanted to be with him, I still communicated with him. I still saw him whenever I could.

PHYSICAL TIES

In 2006 I had my foot surgery. I was out for two months recuperating. Barely able to walk, I still managed to engage with him. Interesting how you can talk to someone but you really don't know who they are or what they are doing. He came back to Houston and called me. Even though I was unable to have full functionality of my left foot, I hobbled out of bed, got dressed and met him at the hotel. Again another wonderful time. I needed to see him. I needed to feel him and touch him.

If he could only understand how I felt about him. We were there for a couple of hours and the time spent was just heaven to me. We made provisions for the bad foot... but we got it all in. "Time well spent, I needed that! It was my stress reliever." I said to myself. I came back home with a smile on my face. I loved him! I really loved him!!! I wanted to spend all of my time with him. Honey, I was on top of the world. I went to work as if I ran the company. My head held high. I had a pep in my step and a glide in my stride. I had it all, really! I finally got the man. Thank you Lord. He was a good man. He had his own business, his own car, his own money. Now, having his own was a big plus. And he was not just good looking, but great looking. Those pecs, those thighs, the biceps, the ripped six-pack abs.

What more can a woman ask for? My life was now complete, or so I thought. I started telling him how much more I wanted to see him. And how I can't wait till he moves to Houston. He never said anything different. He allowed me to believe he was coming here to live. As time went on, he never moved to Houston. He decided to move to Atlanta, Georgia. I was heartbroken but, it didn't stop me from wanting him. Here comes this same little voice (the Holy Spirit) in my head, "When are you going to get enough? When are you going to stop? This is not good for you. He's not trustworthy." It still didn't stop me. I continued on even after the disappointment.

Worksheet

List some Soul-Ties you feel you have with people. They can be Physical, Mental, Emotional and Spiritual. Whatever comes to your mind, write it down.

Area for Extra Notes

The Demand

The more I talked to him, the more time I wanted to be with him. I started telling him he should visit more. I told him I wanted to see him more. Why did I say that? All of a sudden, the frequency of the calls decreased. I didn't hear from him every day like I normally would. A day was missed here and there. Then it started to be several days I would not hear from him. He would not answer my calls nor return them. What was going on! I just couldn't figure it out. It was like all of a sudden he's avoiding me. WOW!!! What did I do? I only asked for more time and told him I wanted to be with him more.

Making demands on a guy will get you hurt big time if you have fallen him. I starting thinking about a lot of things that transpired over the past several years. I changed a lot. I became someone I never wanted to be. I became an angry woman who would get mad and try to get even because things did not work the way I wanted them to. He was supposed to be all into me like I was with him. But now thinking about it, he only acted in response to what I said to him. For instance, if I said, "I love you!" He would respond he loved me back, but only as a response. Thinking, now I feel like a fool.

I feel used. The nerve!!! What right did he have to use me, get what he wanted then when he's ready to move around, he just does? That's not right! And it's unfair! I became so angry, I was bursting at the seams. I wanted revenge. I wanted to get him back really bad. What can I do? What can I say? Dang it!!!

The next morning, I get to work and began listening to my voicemails. There is one from a woman, threatening me not to call him anymore. Well I'll be John Brown. What in the world? Who is this woman? Continuing to listen, she's calling me everything but a child of God. Close to the end of the call she's telling him to tell me not to call him anymore. He, like a parrot, repeated what she said. Now I'm really pissed. My whole day was ruined. First of all, what is she doing calling my work number?!! Second, how did she get my number?!! I was too through. So I called his number back, the woman answered. I informed her, I didn't know he was involved with someone. He never indicated to me he was in a relationship. Instead of screaming, hollering and cursing at her, I told her I did not want any trouble and I hope they have a nice life. Later that day, after I had calmed down, I sent him a text and told him not to call me or email me ever again, and I meant that. How can a person be ok playing with someone's emotions. I was so into him. Apparently, he was not that into me.

The next day, Saturday, I was sitting in my living room drinking some wine coolers. Remember, I had told him not to contact me by phone or email again.

Well, he made a mistake and sent me an email. Why did he do that? My anger and hurt rose up in me so I responded to the email. I hit reply all so everyone he had on the email could read what I said. Then I let him have it.

I cursed him from the crown of his head to the souls of his feet. I called him everything but a child of God. Yea, I was pretty pissed. Here is what I wrote:

> *"Chauncey, I emphatically told you not to call me, text me or email me and you did it anyway. Now you're going to get it. You are a worthless piece of crap and sad wannabe player. You don't even know how to play and not get*

caught. You play on women emotions and think it's ok. You need to learn how to leave people alone when they tell you to. It is sad you think you are getting away with having women all over the place. You will be caught and someone is going to kick your ass. You need a special encounter with Jesus in a major way. You are a poor ass excuse for a man. You think you can make it on your looks but you will get yours in the end. You are a liar and a cheat. Do not ever call me or text me or write me again. I'm going to repeat it again because you didn't hear it the first time I told you. Stay out of my life!"

When I hit the send button, a few minutes later another woman sent an email with a response to all. She stated since I started the train, she was jumping on it also. She cursed him in her email also. Then another woman and another. All these women sending emails jumping on the bandwagon telling him what he was. Ha! So I wasn't the only one he had been messing with and over. All of a sudden I get a call from him. Oh, now he can call and wants to talk? I sent him to voicemail. He called again and again. When I finally picked up, he started screaming through the phone asking me what did I do. I responded in a very calm tone, "What do you mean, what did I do?" He started whining of how I sent the email to everyone and I had just messed up his reputation (As if I cared about his reputation.).

Of course I played dumb and told him I had been drinking and didn't know what I was doing. Then I calmly said, "I told you not to contact me anymore." Then I hung up. Who had I become? This was crazy! This anger and madness! I had to get away from him. He was making me crazy. I had to get out of whatever this was.

The Hurt

A year had passed, it's 2007. I was online doing some research and saw him online. I saw a picture of him and he was in a tuxedo with a beach back ground. I had this sinking feeling in the pit of my stomach. You know, you can tell wedding pictures from regular pictures. My mind started wondering, my thoughts were all over the place. But I had to know. So I asked him if he was married. He hesitated for a minute and finally said yes. My heart sunk. Tears started rolling down my face. I could not stop crying. Oh My God, why is this affecting me now? It's been a year since we've communicated.

He asked if I was okay. My world came crashing down. HE'S MARRIED!!! I couldn't believe it. I didn't want to believe it. I felt like someone just stabbed me in my heart. He went and married some other girl, then moved to Atlanta, Georgia. He had bought a house and cars. That should have been mine. All in a year's time? What the hell!!! He must have been seeing her while he was doing me. I was furious, I'm was mad as hell, Yet, I was so hurt, I couldn't function. I was more hurt than angry. When anger and hurt meet, it is not a good feeling. Where does he get off playing with people emotions? You Bastard!!! All this time you had another family but never had the balls to tell me. His response was, "I didn't know how to tell you". What a sorry ass excuse. All he had to do was just tell me. Had I not confronted him, he probably would not have said anything.

Why in the hell do men play with women's emotions? As long as they can get what they want, they won't say a word. They try to play two or more women at the same time thinking it won't catch up with them. Not to mention the danger of having so many sex partners. What's done in the dark will come to the light eventually. They play dumb founded when they get caught and confronted. Then they want to turn everything around on you trying to say, you're the reason I cheated or you made me do it. LIES, LIES, and more LIES!!!! No one makes you go out and do anything you don't already want to do. All these years of talking and visiting. I was just somewhat entertainment for him. Hurt and anger together is a killer.

I felt so guilty and ashamed. I felt like I was the sidekick. Damn It!!! How could I allow someone to use me like this. I know I'm better than this. I've always been the girl who tell other women, not to let a man use them. HA! And I was the very one who got used. I got played for years. I let my guard down because I thought he was real. I was fooled by the outer appearance: a sexy body, a mesmerizing smile and a handsome face. Oh and don't forget the words, he spoke the right words at the right time. The hurt and pain of being betrayed and deceived was too much to bear. I could not function for a long time. I withdrew from everyone. My family, my friends, even my church family. I started wearing dark colors because my soul was darken by all of this. The same voice (the Holy Spirit) which had been with me came back and said, "I told you this was not good for you. I've been saying this for years. You knew in your spirit this was not right." I had no more contact with him after this confession. It took me years to get over him, or so I thought. He hurt me to my core. It was almost impossible to love another man or even want to love again. My heart was sealed with him inside and it would take supernatural surgery from God above to remove him.

The feeling of not having a man in my life was over whelming. I didn't want to be by myself again. This lonely feeling can take you places you don't want to go. I cried for a long time. I guess I needed to get it out of me. Some days were better than others. But then some days, I couldn't eat, I couldn't sleep, I didn't want to do anything. I wanted this feeling to just disappear. The feeling of anger, the feeling of sadness, the feeling of being used, the feeling of guilt and shame. The feeling of how I was disobedient to God. All of it! Just go away and leave me alone. I never thought I would be in this deep. I fell in love with this guy.

I had to admit it to myself I was actually in love with him. I felt guilty and ashamed because I allowed him to use me. I was used for years, my spirit knew it but my flesh didn't want to hear it. All he had to do was say the right words and I forgave him. A part of me wanted to get back at him. But it wasn't my character to seek revenge. I wanted to hurt him like he hurt me. To make him feel what I was feeling but how could I? He's gone on with his life and I'm sitting here, sulking and pouting, tripping emotionally. What can I do? I need to get up, dust the dirt off of myself and get back in the game. "There are better men out there than this one." I said to myself. "I've got to keep it moving. I am in control of my destiny." No one else can really come into my life until I release the clutter in my heart regarding this guy. I've got to get better. I can't let anyone take me out like this. I can't let a man be my down fall.

"I am better than this." I said to myself. I am a woman with goals and dreams. I must get up and fight these emotions. I am a winner. I am a survivor.

I can beat this. I can do this. I can do all things through Christ that gives me strength. What's interesting is you can't truly serve the Lord and Worship Him when you have sin and mess going on in your life. You can go to church all you want but if your mess is still there, lingering around, it will be hard to lift your hands in praise and worship. Man, the devil played a really good trick on me. And I let him. Not anymore!

> ***Deuteronomy 28:13 - 13** And the LORD shall make thee the head, and not the tail; and thou shalt be above only, and thou shalt not be beneath; if that thou hearken unto the commandments of the LORD thy God,*

which I command thee this day, to observe and to do them:

Philippians 4:13   *I can do all things through Christ which strengtheneth me.*

The Compromise

Several years have passed and it's now 2012. Life was good. I'm focused on my career. I'm now traveling for the company. All was well. I'm traveling to places I would never had thought to visit. My first trip was to Columbus, OH. I was there for one week. Working myself to the bone. Working overnight and sleeping during the day. I had to keep mind preoccupied. Every once in a while the thought of him would enter my mind. I had to push it out of the way. I hadn't talked to him since 2007. Since I found out he was married. I had gotten a better grip on my feelings and emotions. Out of sight out of mind. Later on in the year, I got a call out of the clear blue sky. Damn It! It was him. What in the hell does he want. He just wanted to talk. RIGHT!!! I answered my phone, he asked how I was doing. He asked what was going on with me and I told him I've been keeping myself busy traveling with the company. We chatted for a few minutes and I was doing great. No emotions involved. I made a mistake and told him I had a trip to Springfield, MO. with a layover in Atlanta. He asked if he could meet me at the airport. I just knew I had my emotions under control. I told him it was fine. First mistake. I told him I had about an hour and a half. Even though the layover was three hours, he didn't need to know. So the trip was in October 2012. I told him when my plane was going to land. When my flight landed, sure enough he was there waiting!

I walked to his car and got in. I told him I was on a time restraint and didn't want to miss my connecting flight. So, he pulled into the parking garage and we talked. He was truly admiring me, telling me how beautiful I was. Remember the words they say? They know what to say at the right time. I was dressed to impress! He gave me a hug and told me I smelled really good. Then he kissed me. Oh hell!!! How could I fall for this again? The feelings and emotions came rushing back in as if they had never left. One thing led to another and we ended up having sex again, in the back seat of his car. So many things were running through my head. Like:

what the hell am I doing? Are you crazy? Then I started compromising. I don't have to see him all the time. A fix here and there. Once a year. It will be okay. When we were done, he took me back to the terminal. Looking all starry-eyed he said, "I have really missed you. And you really look great!" Yep, I know I looked good. That was on purpose. Yes, he had protection. I would never do anything without it.

I caught my flight and went on to Springfield. On the flight, all I could think about was what happened. How was I feeling? How was he feeling? What did this mean? It was good though. I figured, I'm a grown woman. I can do whatever I wanted to do, or so I thought. I psyched myself up saying, "I can handle this". I will not get emotional over this.

Well, it a lie from the pit of hell. My feelings got all involved and wrapped up again. I compromised and said I can use him for a fix like he used me. Any time I had a chance to go to or fly into Atlanta, I went. My inner voice didn't say anything to me this time, strange.

I couldn't wait to see him again. In 2013, I had another project in Atlanta I stayed for several days. Yep, I told him I was going to be there for a few days. I told him the name of the hotel and what time the plane was landing. Two hours after I land, he showed up at the hotel. I got my fix and I was good. Unbeknownst to me, the soul ties were still there. I thought I had gotten rid of them during the time of not seeing or speaking to him. The only thing happen was I pushed it out of my head and preoccupied my mind with other stuff. These ties were stronger than before. I finished the work for my project and came back home. Here I go again, getting back into the same craziness. Still no voice. Okay something is not right.

A year later, in August 2014, I had another trip to Atlanta. Again, I told him about it. I told him I wanted him to stay longer than he normally would. He asked me how long I wanted him to stay, I told him at least three hours. When the time came for me to leave, I flew in early because I had a big surprise for him. I decorated the room with candles, rose petals on the bed and the floor. I created a trail from the door to the bed. I had a bottle of champagne on ice and created a playlist of soft love songs I liked. I prepared myself to knock his socks off. I wanted to show him what he was really missing. He knocked on the door, I had a wireless speaker on the nightstand. I opened the door, and pressed play. The music started, the lights were out and the candles were flickering. He walked through the hallway into the room in AWE!!! His bag dropped and he grabbed me and kissed me like never before. I wooed him in a way no woman has ever done before. For the first time, we made love. Hour after hour after hour, it was wonderful!!! He wanted to talk, I wanted to take a nap. But I stayed up and talked with him. Then of course, he started complaining of a tooth ache. What the hell!!! Why it was all of a sudden you now have a toothache.

Laying there trying to find a dentist, really? When did he know he had a toothache? Before he showed up to the hotel? Or after we had sex and he had to leave. Yep, you guessed it, he left. When I looked at the time, it was exactly three hours. It is amazing how a guy can manipulate you. It was all about the sex. I compromised and again allowed him to come into my life. I had to accept the fact, he never loved me like I loved him. I had to accept the fact, nothing was going to change. I had to accept the fact when I asked him if he was still married, he said yes. Even though he continued to play this game, I still compromised. I still allowed the communication to go on.

After the project was over, I came home. He called me several times a day. Talking about what I had done for him. He told me how he's thought about it every day since then. All of a sudden, November rolls around and the calls get less frequent. December comes, their even less. Didn't hear from him during the Christmas holiday. Hmmm, no call, no text, no nothing. Okay! Here we go again the same crap. Why did I let myself fall into this again? How could I? Accepting the truth of the matter was a reality call. I was the side-chick. Apparently, it had always been that way, and a bad place to be. A side-chick never gets anything of value. A side-chick doesn't get to spend holidays. A Side-chick doesn't get the gifts for your birthday, Valentine's Day or Christmas. You will always be second best. I see it, truly see it, and have accepted it. It will never be what I had envisioned. It will just never be.

Worksheet

On this worksheet, list the things that the individual have done on the left side and how it made you feel on the right side. The reason for this is to get your emotions down on paper and out of you.

What they did to you	How it made you feel

BREAK OUT!   Regina J. King

Area for Extra Notes

_____

Leaving for Good

I have to get out of this. It's not good for me, nor is it healthy. The emotional roller-coaster is turning my life upside down. Feeling like I mattered to him, then feeling like I didn't. I have to make a decision. Do I want to continue this? It will always be on his terms. I would have to go where he is located. I would have to spend my money. He'll never buy anything, no airline ticket, no hotel room, no car rental, nothing. I have to break out of this cycle. All of this is going through my mind. What do I really want to do?

In March 2015, I went to Atlanta for a conference for my business. Of course, I told him I was going to be there. I was still torn on what to do. Yet, my feelings were not as strong about him as they had been over the past several years. Upon arriving, I checked into the hotel and got started with the conference. He started texting me asking when I will be finished. I told him I would text him when it was about over. When I found out what time it was over, I texted him and told him it wasn't going to be over until 11:30pm. He wanted to come by then but would not be able to stay that long. I'm thinking, it would be a booty call. You come get what you want and then you are out of the door. No quality time spent, it's just a wham bam, thank you ma'am. So I told him no, it was going to be too late.

He asked if he could come the early the next morning. I told him yes. I got up early Saturday morning and prepared the room. He was supposed to be there at 6am because the meeting started at 8am. Well, 6am rolled around and left, no sign of Mr. Chauncey. In my frustration, I got dressed and went to the conference. He decides to text me at 7:55am as if nothing happened. I waited a few hours and responded, by this time I was pissed. He asked me if I was on break and I told him NO! The conference let out at about 5:30pm. So I texted him and told him I was done. He responded he could not come at that time but he will come. I decided to go out to get some dinner from this great restaurant called Marietta Diner and returned to the hotel. I had a good ole time eating and relaxing. I received a text from him asking if I was back in my room. I said yes and no. I told him I was at the hotel but not in my room. I was in the lounge in the hotel lobby hanging out with some people I met at the conference. (Remember, I was in my room, in my bed but I wasn't telling him that). He stated he could come now but couldn't stay too long. When he said those words, I instantly got angry and told him just don't bother.

I was ready to go to sleep and I got a text message from him asking who was with me and was I screwing them. First of all, he didn't have a right to ask this. Secondly, it was not any of his business if I was with someone, although I was not, I was on my way to sleep. Then he pops an attitude like a little girl, telling me he wasn't stupid and for me to remember he's not. Another text message came and said not to text him back. Okay, this has now sent me over the edge. I messaged back and told him, "It's amazing what you really think of me. It's very shallow of you. I am done! So done!!!"

Sunday morning came, I checked out of my hotel and headed to the airport. Sitting there at the gate I started thinking about all of this stuff going on in my life. During the flight, I thought about what transpired during the weekend. Many emotions surfaced. I was ecstatic about what I learned in the conference, I was pissed about the way Chauncey acted. Then a feeling of sadness because I knew I needed to separate from him. I made it back home safely. I'm thinking, what a trip. I mean both figuratively and literally. I decided to cut him cold turkey. No communication, no texting, no email, no nothing. I was so tired of being used. I was the one who was always on the losing end of this whatever you want to call it, relationship, I guess. No, it's not a relationship. I don't know what it was. But, whatever it was, I have to get out of it. My anger at him allowed me to go a good month without speaking to him. Then all of a sudden, I started thinking about him. I wanted to talk to him, talk about what happened. He didn't return my text messages, my phone calls, and my messages on Facebook. No response from anything I sent him. I went to my best friend and cried on her shoulder.

She was not one to sugar coat anything. She was brutally honest, and told me that I was part of the blame for what happened. Okay, I looked at her like she was crazy, and asked her, "What you mean?" She said,

> "Well, you made him think you were with someone else and you were not. You should have just told him the truth that you were tired and were already in the bed. But instead you made it seem like you were having a good time with other people." Then she stated, "You see, men have a one track mind. Meaning, it doesn't matter what they do, they can be with one woman one

hour and go be with another one the next hour. But in their heads, if you belong to them, you are not supposed to be with any other man, period. If you tell them you are hanging out with a friend, they will automatically think that means you are with a man and that you are screwing him. They have a double standard when it comes to women."

Lastly, she said, "If you want him back, you will have to do some begging. Because right now, he's very pissed at you and doesn't want to talk to you. So you will have to apologize for everything that happened and take the blame for it all. Now on the other hand, if you want to be done with him, then leave it alone and go your way. But you need to figure out what you want." Boy, was that a reality check. My crying on her shoulder stopped and she sent me back to my desk making me think about what she said.

A few days went by. I went back to her office because I had time to think about what she said. I told her I wanted him back. Although, I should not want him back, right, because it's not good and it's wrong. She told me if I wanted him back then apologize. I sat in her office and text him this message:

"Chauncey, I love you and can't stop thinking about you. This trip was a botched trip and I want to make it up to you. This trip took more of my time than I could have ever expected. There were a few missteps on both of our parts and I think we should talk about it and work through this. There has never been one who had my heart or will ever have my heart quite like you. Let's make up. I heard makeup sex is the absolute best. What do you think?"

After I sent the text, he still didn't respond. Okay now, my heart is really distraught. I am wondering what I am going to do. Why is he not responding, I apologized. This has taken total control of me. I'm not functioning well. I am having crying spells on my job. I'm trying to hide it but it doesn't work. As time goes on, I'm trying to rationalize this thing. I'm trying to get him out of my system. It's the end of March, I'm out to lunch with my bestie, and she asked if he responded, I told her no. So she said to call him. I told her he won't pick up. She said call anyway and she will leave a voicemail. So I called and gave her the phone, it went to voicemail as I expected. She grabbed the phone, told him it was her and started speaking. After her long spill, she hung up. The next day, he responded with a text message and stated he wasn't talking to me at the moment. We both started laughing and then she said, "The ball is in his court. You will have to wait this out."

Now it's the beginning of May. I have really begun to get him out of my system. So, I thought. I've cried, I've been depressed and now I feel like I'm on the upside of this turmoil. I feel better. My emotions are stable now and I no longer have crying fits. You know, the ones that keep you up at night and make your eyes puffy and bloodshot. Yes, those fits. I am really in a good place. You know, the devil always try to put a stopper in your way. I said I was feeling really good now, and all of a sudden I get a text message from him. He texted me asking what was I doing for the weekend. He wanted to let me know he would be in Baton Rouge. Now, remember, we haven't talked since March. I responded with a hello and told him I would be unavailable for the weekend. I was going car shopping. Now he wants to strike up a conversation. I am emotionally detached. The conversation is the same thing. So I chatted via text message but it was very nonchalant. I was just tired and through with him. By this time, I started filling my thoughts with new things. Changing what I was thinking. I started focusing on what was happening to me. During the summer, I was going to lose my job. I needed to figure out what the next phase of my life would be. The company was going through a site strategy and location strategy phase. In layman terms, they were in the process of laying people off. I needed to start taking this seriously, and not worry about a man who never had me in his heart as his number one. Had he, we would have been married and he would not be with someone else. I decided I didn't need him in my life and started to treat him with a nonchalant attitude. I put forth no effort to contact him. If I communicated with him, it was because he initiated it. I needed to turn my life around. I realized God never left me. I left Him. I needed to go back to where He was waiting for me. I was thankful that God loved me enough to give me another chance. Even in my sin, God had angels take charge over my life even while doing the crazy stuff I was doing, God protected me.

***Romans 12:1-2** - 1 I beseech you therefore, brethren, by the mercies of God, that ye present your bodies a living sacrifice, holy, acceptable unto God, which is your reasonable service.*

2 And be not conformed to this world: but be ye transformed by the renewing of your mind, that ye may prove what is that good, and acceptable, and perfect, will of God.

Worksheet

List some things you can do to prepare yourself to leave this situation for good.

BREAK OUT!   Regina J. King

Area for Extra Notes

Pack Your Emotional Bags and Go!

At the beginning of the year, I got the notice that my job was relocating. I had a choice to move to: Columbus, OH; Garden City, NY; Delaware, NJ; Tampa, FL or Dallas, TX or lose my job. I purchased my house in 2003 and was almost through paying for it. Now, they want me to uproot everything I have and move someplace else just to keep my job. None of those places were conducive for me. At this time of my life, starting over was not an option. My family was here, my friends, my church family. Everything I've known is here in

Houston. This was a lot for me to deal with emotionally. I have to do what I have to do.

As the summer continued, I was preparing to leave my job. I was slowly but surely taking my stuff home being inconspicuous to everyone. As the middle of August rolled around, and then my last day at work, my emotions were in a knot. I was leaving everyone and everything I knew for the last 15 years. I did something I had never done working there, I wore a dress with heels. It was funny because most people did not recognize me. I said my goodbyes to everyone who meant something to me. As I was saying bye to people, my best friend told me to come to her office because she needed help with her computer. When I got there, she asked me to fix the computer in the conference room. So we walk to the room and I opened the door. OMG!!! To my surprise, there were

a group of colleagues, former managers and friends hiding in the room. They had it decorated beautifully. There was food, gifts, etc. Her employees put together a going away party for me, it was so emotional. They had a whole little program for me. They all spoke and expressed how much I had touched their lives and what I meant to them. If I never knew I was loved, I knew that day.

Everyone cried including my former boss and best friend. When the day was over, my heart was heavy because I knew I would not be coming back to work there. I knew I would not be able to talk to the people like I had for so many years. I knew my friendships was going to change and a strain was going to be there. It is one thing when you have access to someone and another thing when you don't. The pressure of staying friends was on. One more set of hurts I had to deal with.

The only guy I really had in my life had one foot out of the door and the other on a banana peel. Losing my job, and now dealing with fighting to keep my friendship with my best friend, is a lot. What more can this emotional rollercoaster offer? It's like a ride that doesn't stop. But I have to make it stop. I have to move forward. It's the end of one chapter and the beginning of a new one. The issue was I don't know what the new chapter was supposed to be.

All this time, I have been praying and asking God for direction. I knew I needed guidance from the Holy Spirit. He had been talking to me all these years and when He went silent, I was lost. I had to really begin to seek the Lord because my life was traveling an unknown path. The emotions, the job, the worry set in and I got depressed. My soul tie with Chauncey was so powerful because I did not realize I was not only tied to him, I was also tied to every other person he had been with. This spiritual force is real and nothing to play with. I had been mentally, emotionally, physically, and spiritually tied to this guy for sixteen years. Sometimes you put in so much time with a person that leaving is not an option. Those are years I will never be able to restore. They are gone forever. That was a third of my life gone because of this ungodly relationship.

Enough time wasted, it was time to make a decision to pick up my emotional bags and go or stay on this crazy rollercoaster ride. I wanted more from the Lord. My desire was to be with God. I wanted to do His will but could not because of the baggage I was carrying. Sin will keep you from entering into God's place of rest. I wanted the joy and peace I once had. I had it when I was serving the Lord. I made the decision, I chose to stop dealing with Chauncey and cut him off cold turkey. Please believe me, it was no easy task. Songs and places would try and remind me of him. Thank God he never came to my house. That would have been a major problem. The devil wants you to stay in the mess you are in because he has the opportunity to keep you down and out of God's will. When you make a decision to live for Jesus Christ, you have to leave all that you know and begin a new life in Him. If you straddle the fence, you will never be all that God wants you to be and you will never receive what He has in store for you.

***Hebrews 13:5-6** - 5 Let your conversation be without covetousness; and be content with such things as ye have: for he hath said, I will never leave thee, nor forsake thee. 6 So that we may boldly say, The Lord is my* *helper, and I will not fear what man shall do unto me.*

Soul-Ties

I've been off work for two months now, and I've been resting and reflecting on who I've become over the past several years. I had become a functioning depressed person. Most people would not have known this because I hid it so well. I walked around as if I had it all together. Being quick to help others in their crisis but I was suffering with mine. I did not like who I had become over the years.

I had developed an attitude problem. When things didn't go my way, I would become would become angry with people quickly. I would stop talking to people just because then told me "no". I had developed a short temper and would get angry over the smallest thing. Let someone say something to me and I didn't like it, I would flip off at the mouth depending on who it was, of course. All of this was never a part of my character. I basically started living a lie. I had become someone else. I did things I said I would never do. Remember the soul-ties I talked about earlier those spirits are real. A soul tie is a link between two people in the soul and spirit realm. It links their souls together which can bring forth beneficial results or negative results.

Thinking about everything that transpired in my life with this guy, I realized the soul tie had taken control. And it brought forth negative results in my life. They didn't seem negative at the time but, they were. The devil can use soul-ties to take advantage of you.

The devil can use soul ties to make you believe something that is not real and give you a false sense of security. They are formed from having sex outside of marriage and cause a person to become defiled. In the book of

> ***Genesis 34:2-3*** *- 2 And when Shechem the son of Hamor the Hivite, prince of the country, saw her, he took her, and lay with her, and defiled her. 3 And his soul clave unto Dinah the daughter of Jacob, and he loved the damsel, and spake kindly unto the damsel.*

It talks about a prince named Shechem. He saw a woman he wanted, took her and had sex with her. The problem was she was not his wife. Now, because of his sin, he was tied to her and she was tied to him.

This is why it is so easy and so common for a man or a woman to still have feelings toward their ex-lovers. They know they should not still have an attraction but they do. Even years later, there are still some signs of emotions there. You can be married or developing a relationship with someone else but those feelings are still there. Most times they show up at the most inopportune time. You'll hear a song and it would remind you of a memory you shared with the individual. Or a place you go to or see, it's a reminder of what you did with that person. All of this is because of ungodly soul ties. You see, demonic spirits can take advantage of these types of soul ties and use it to transfer spirits from person to person. Yes, this stuff is real! You have to get rid of all ungodly soul ties past and present. It will destroy you if you don't. Now if you married the person you had that tie with, that's a little different. That's how I got in the condition I was in. Those soul ties isolated me from others, even people in the church.

I had started trying to deal with things on my own. I had stopped praying like I used to. It had become burdensome to go to church because I knew my spirit was not right. I couldn't praise or worship God like I knew I could. I knew I had issues. The devil had me all intertwined with this guy. And it all started when I became defiled with him sixteen years ago. So yes, I had changed and it wasn't for the good.

I had to get past this and truly move forward. I had to get my mind right. The first thing I had to do was finally stop all communication. Shut the doors that could possibly allow him to contact me. Next I prayed, repented, and asked God to forgive me for the wrong, and the role I had played in this relationship. After that, I renounced the soul-tie. I said a prayer like this: "In Jesus' name, I now renounce any ungodly soul ties formed between myself and _____ as a result of _____ (fornication, etc.)."

Then I prayed to break the soul-tie: "I now break and sever any ungodly soul ties formed between myself and _____ as a result of _____ (fornication, etc.) in Jesus' name." In the blanks, place the name of the person and the bond or sin you had this that person.

Next, I had to forgive myself for what I done. You know, one of the most difficult things to do is to forgive yourself. It's already hard enough to forgive those who have done something to you. But much harder to forgive you for what you've done to yourself. You see, forgiveness is not so much for the person or people that wrong you, it's for you. It's to release you so that the guilt and shame won't consume you. Because if you don't forgive, it will consume you. You will be trapped in a world of bitterness and possibly hatred. When you pray, and you are sincere, Christ forgives you right then and there. So forgive yourself and forgive others.

> ***Matthew 6: 14-15*** - *14 For if ye forgive men their trespasses, your heavenly Father will also forgive you: 15 But if ye forgive not men their trespasses, neither will your Father forgive your trespasses.*

Worksheet

Make a list of things and relationships that you have soul-ties with. Then pray the prayer above and insert this list to renounce them out of your life.

Area for Extra Notes

I Choose Me

After following the steps of getting my spirit right. I was able to start loving me more and allowing God to love me again. I had a different outlook on life. I felt like I could live again. There was a light at the end of my tunnel. I started doing things for myself. I stopped looking for someone to be in my life and started spending time with me and the Lord. Does any of this make sense? I began doing things I liked to do. I started dressing different. I used to wear dark colors because that's how I was feeling inside. I wore them because my soul was a little dark. My spirit was troubled. But now, I can see. I can see clearly now the rain is gone... I had a new lease on life. I had a different outlook. I chose me. I started caring for me. I took time out to become reacquainted with myself. I started going out to eat again. Just doing activities that were fun and made me happy. I began developing new friendships with people who truly wanted to be my friend, and not for what I could do for them. I became more active in church and more talkative. I started going to workshops and seminars to better myself.

> ***2 Corinthians 5:17*** - *17 Therefore if any man be in Christ, he is a new creature: old things are passed away; behold, all things are become new.*

The work started in me and now it is coming out of me. When I took the interest in myself, I began writing my dreams down again. The goals I had for my life came alive again. As I wrote things down regarding what I wanted to accomplish, more things started to come to mind. It was like God had open the flood gates to my mind and things started to happen. Things were coming together quickly. I started teaching Sunday school better than ever. It had meaning now. Not that it didn't before but, now I was teaching with power and authority.

There's something you must understand about leaders in the church. They have struggles too. They will perpetrate a fraud because they don't want to be look down on or frowned at. One thing is true, you cannot minister to people if you are not willing to be real and be ministered to. You have to let the people know you have issues also. The issues can be with your family, relationships or even within yourself. If more people would be real, more people would come to church and get saved. You see, the church is like a hospital. Hurt people come there to get help and to get healed. Let the church get real, please. That is one thing I promised I would do, be real with folks. We all have struggles. We all deal with storms. Either we are in the middle of one, just coming out of one, or about to go into one. No one is exempt. Not the pastors, not the preachers, not the singers, not the deacons, not the elders, no one.

__Romans 3:23 - 23__ "For all have sinned, and come short of the glory of God."

No one can point the finger at another to illuminate their sin. There is no sin greater than the other. That's why we need God's help. We need Jesus in our lives. We need him as Lord and Saviour.

Because I had rededicated my life back to Christ, my flow was back. Things started working together for the good. I had to prioritize what I wanted to do first. Then I started walking in faith and began to achieve them. I prayed and asked God to send someone into my life to teach me the things that He wanted me to learn and know. And he blessed me with a woman of God who showed up with some serious power and authority.

Her name is Apostle Gloria J. Little. She became a part of my church over a year ago. She started coming to my Sunday school class. She introduced herself to me in November 2015. She was different, she was truly a Godsend. The first time we had an actual conversation was January 17th, 2016. We were asked by the Bishop to help at a funeral at church. We showed up in obedience read the scripture and did the prayer. I had an 11am appointment that I pushed back to 2pm. When the service was over, we were asked if we were going to the gravesite. I told Bishop I could not because I had a previous appointment. Apostle Little responded and said "No." I looked at her waiting for the explanation but one never came. I asked myself, who is this woman who dares to say no to Bishop? She said to me, "You should never be forced to do something you don't want to do." She made a good point. She then stated, "A workman is worthy of his hire."

Luke 10:7 - 7 And in the same house remain, eating and drinking such things as they give: for the labourer is worthy of his hire. Go not from house to house.

This was the pivotal point in my life. From that day, I told her she was sent here by God to help me get to where God wants me. Everyone should have an angel in their lives to teach them and show them the way. As I talked to her, she started sharing some things from a spiritual standpoint as well as a business avenue. This woman was a breath of fresh air. I knew I needed to surround myself with God-hearted people. They had a true love for God and a mindset to own businesses. This woman of God taught me so much in the short months I've been with her than I have learned in years. She begin to educate me about having my own. She taught me how to stop letting people run over me. She taught me how to be stronger spiritually, emotionally as well as mentally. She taught me it was okay to say, "NO!" You see, <u>God does answer prayers. He does hear you</u>. She led by example and showed me in addition to telling me what needed to be done. She told me if I was really ready for God to make a change, there were a few things I still needed to do.

I informed her that Chauncey wanted to do the cover for my book. When I told her that, Apostle nearly hit the ceiling. She stated, "Are you still talking to him?" I said, "Yes! But nothing was going on. We aren't doing anything." She said, "Oh, well, you're not ready." I told her I was and needed this change in my life. She mentioned, "You need to cut all communications with this dude. Delete his number, the whole nine yards". I asked about the pictures. She said, "Everything pertaining to him. You still have him going around with you because he is still in your phone. He goes everywhere you go. You have to let it go". Boy that was a wakeup call. I never thought about the residue of him still being tied to me because he was in my phone. While I was on the phone talking to her, I went through my phone and deleted every picture I had of him. I deleted his phone numbers and contact. Any memory I had of him, I got rid of it. Even the text messages. I had every text message he ever sent me. I had to delete them also. I tell you, this was not an easy task. It was hard as hell. I felt my heart palpitating fast. My hands started to sweat, I became extremely nervous. But I did it! Then I told her while still on the phone, I deleted everything. I deleted the pictures, the text messages, his numbers and contact information. You see, if you want to have the power of God working in your life, there are some things you must do. You have to make the decision to BREAK OUT. Break out of bad relationships! Break out of bad friendships! Break Out of low self-esteem! Break Out of a poverty mindset! Break out of the pity parties! Break out of the woe it's me syndrome! You have to Break Out by any means necessary. You also have to want to break out of your current situation. People are praying for you. People you don't even know. I am praying for you. It is not easy when you have been conditioned for so long. You take a step every day to heal from your past hurts. The first thing you have to do is acknowledge your hurt. You have to make a list of them. If the devil can make you continue to deny your feelings, he can continue to hold that over your head.

> ***John 10:10*** *- 10 The thief cometh not, but for to steal, and to kill, and to destroy: I am come that they might have life, and that they might have it more abundantly.*

Next, pray and ask God to forgive you and heal you from your past hurts.

> *1 John 1:9* - *9 If we confess our sins, he is faithful and just to forgive us our sins, and to cleanse us from all unrighteousness.*

Next, you must trust and believe that you are forgiven and begin walking in your new life.

> *Romans 7:6* - *6 But now we are delivered from the law, that being dead wherein we were held; that we should serve in newness of spirit, and not in the oldness of the letter.*

Make it a point every day to think positive about yourself. You are more than a conqueror. Your life was predestined by God.

> ***Romans 8:37*** *- 37 Nay, in all these things we are more than conquerors through him that loved us.*
>
> ***1 Peter 2:9*** *- 9 But ye are a chosen generation, a royal priesthood, an holy nation, a peculiar people; that ye should shew forth the praises of him who hath called you out of darkness into his marvelous light:*
>
> ***Romans 8 28-31*** *- 28 And we know that all things work together for good to them that love God, to them who are*

the called according to his purpose. 29 For whom he did foreknow, he also did predestinate to be conformed to the image of his Son, that he might be the firstborn among many brethren. 30 Moreover whom he did predestinate, them he also called: and whom he called, them he also justified: and whom he justified, them he also glorified. 31 What shall we then say to these things? If God be for us, who can be against us?

BREAK OUT!

Regina J. King

Start Living NOW!

I'm starting my new life and I feel great. I'm taking actions toward my dreams and my goals. Since that time I have developed a new company and also started my ministry. Every day I am taking steps to get closer to my destination. I am working on my desires and am having fun while doing it. Having a new lease on life is a beautiful thing. The peace I have received from God. You know, *"And the peace of God, which passeth all understanding, shall keep your hearts and minds through Christ Jesus."(Philippians 4:7)* The things I am experiencing, words cannot express. I am like a kid in a candy store.

Every day I am thankful for my mind. And I reflect on what I've done to see if I am closer to my accomplishments. Every night, I prepare for what I will do on tomorrow and I plan for it. I thank God for allowing me to get through the day and pray for protection through the night. My life is planned out. And so is yours. You have to want to get out of your current situation and begin the healing process. Will it be easy, no it won't, but it is doable. I started over and so can you. It's all about making a choice, the right choice. Plan your life, one day at a time and ask God to help you. The thing about it is, He will.

I am living my best life now. What a turn around. Sixteen years of time wasted on something you know will never come into fruition, is a lot of time wasted. When you allow God to clean you up, not only does He clean you up but He cleans you from the inside out. I can honestly say I am doing things I've always wanted to do. I had lost the confidence to do them. I not only created my dreams list, my goals list, I've also created a flucket list. (Flucket means fuck it, I'm going to do it now). That is the list you have that has the crazy fun things you want to do and you say, "Forget it, I'm doing them anyway." On my dreams list, I have my fortune 100 company, the ministry, my computer company, my gold company, my travel company, my prepaid card company, etc. On my goals list, I have my commitment to be out of debt by the end of the year. I have to be a millionaire by the end of year. I have my speaking engagements scheduled, etc. Now on my flucket list, I have things like taking a trip to Europe, Zip-lining, parachuting, para-sailing (even though I can't swim), hand gliding, traveling the world. I desire to achieve all that God has for me. I have broken out of my former life and now living my new life.

I am waiting in expectation for God to do what He had promised He would do. If He can do this for me, He can definitely do it for you. You just have to ask Him.

Living in Limbo

I lived in limbo for 16 years of my life. That was 1/3 of my life wasted on someone who would never be with me. I write this story to share with you so you won't have to go through what I've been through. It won't take you as long to get out of your current situation. Don't waste your life on meaningless relationships. When I say relationships, I mean all relationships. It includes friendships as well. Even though they may say the right things to you, or buy you something now and again, that doesn't mean anything anymore. A very wise lady once told me, if your body is telling you something, listen to it. What she meant was, when you come into the person's presence, do you get a sick feeling? Do you feel your blood pressure starting to rise? Do you begin to feel Irritated? Do you get Agitated? What about Sad? Or Depressed? Do you feel worst after talking to him or her when you leave them? Anyone who makes you have any negative emotions/feelings, they need to go. They need to exit stage left. Now don't get me wrong, it won't be easy because they may have been in your life for a long time. Sometimes we have to make decisions that are difficult and we don't want to make them. But, once the negativity is gone from your life, you will feel like a weight has been lifted off your back. Living in limbo is a bad place to be. It is a dark place no one should experience. You don't know what's going to happen to you and you are not in control. You base everything on what the other person may or may not do and say or may not say. You don't want to take time to do something because he or she may call. So you wait, and wait, and wait, and you're still waiting. Why do you have to wait, you really can't call them because they may be with their number one. Yes, I said it. You are not number one and will never be number one. If by chance you get the number one spot, guess what, the number two spot is now open to be filled. You see the cycle? You should not put yourself in that predicament and if you are in that predicament, "Break Out" of it! Get out quickly! I know and understand, it feels good for the moment, but it won't last long or end well.

Last Words

Beloved, are you tired of being in one bad relationship after another? Are you dealing with baggage from a bitter breakup? Are you tired of being miserable and unhappy? If so, this book is for you!

This book is for the individual who will be honest with themselves about their past and, who desires to make a change in their life. You were not created to live a miserable, sad, or pitiful life. "STOP IT!" "STOP!" allowing people to use you. "STOP!" allowing people to abuse you and then throw you away like old underwear. "STOP!" allowing people to lie to you telling you what you want to hear and then do something completely different.

Take a stand and change your life. Get control of your life back. Break Out! is for those who have been hurt in the past by different types of relationships. Do you know the emotions you experience today has something to do with your past, and will hinder your future, it's all related. You allow past hurts to hinder you in everything good this life has to offer. It hinders you from future healthy relationships, from the dream job you desire, from living the good life. Get rid of negative soul-ties. You have to Break Out of the cycle and start living today. It Can Happen For You, <u>NOW</u>!

BREAK OUT!

Regina J. King

BIBLIOGRAPHY

The Holy Bible, King James Version; Thompson Chain Reference Study Bible Copyright, 1903, 1917, 1929,1934, 1957, 1964, 1982 By Frank Charles Thompson

Regina King is a single woman and minister who resides in Houston, Texas. She has experienced God's wonderful mercy and grace in her life. She decided to give God her all and has not turned back. When she gave God her life, He showered her with love and blessings that she didn't have room enough to receive.

Regina J. King Ministries, Inc. was founded by Minister King with a vision to help women and men heal from the hurt of their past. Her mission is to help individuals walk in their deliverance from their past and through personal growth, begin to live the life they were predestined to live. Through teaching and preaching the word of God, she has help countless of individuals start their new journey.

You may contact Minister Regina King through her email address: rking@reginajkingministries.com or visit the website at www.reginajkingministries.com.

For booking engagements, please contact:

It Is Possible, LLC

Email: rking@itispossiblellc.com

Website: www.itispossiblellc.com

BREAK OUT!   Regina J. King

BREAK OUT! Regina J. King

www.ingramcontent.com/pod-product-compliance
Lightning Source LLC
LaVergne TN
LVHW051130080426
835510LV00018B/2338